D1123075

My Body Is Mine!

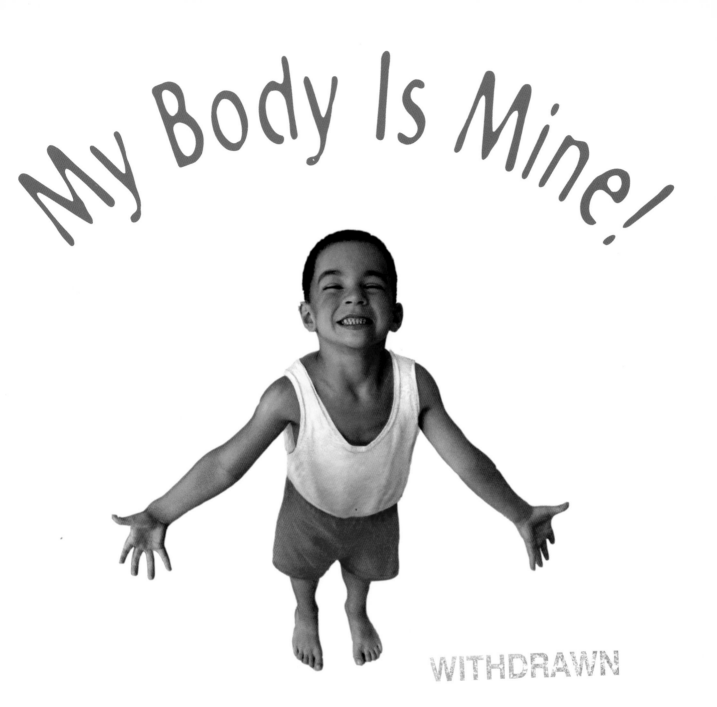

By Peter Osilaja
Illustrated by Gary Phillips

Amandla
PUBLISHING COMPANY

Library of Congress Cataloging-in-Publication Data

is available at the Library of Congress

Text copyright © 2007 Peter Osilaja

Illustrations copyright © 2007 Gary Phillips

Book Design by Kathy Defensor

Published in 2007 by Amandla Publishing Company

for KidSafety of America

17647 Buttercup Court, Chino Hills, CA 91709

www.kidsafetystore.com

ISBN 1-884413-84-6
ISBN 1-884413-83-8

Printed in China

A NOTE TO PARENTS AND CAREGIVERS

Lately, news of a child abused or neglected seems an everyday occurrence. Why? Are we, as a society, reporting it more, or are more children being victimized? It is probably a combination of the two. Internet access and greater public awareness are two reasons for increased news on child abuse and neglect.

Like all forms of abuse, child sexual abuse and exploitation could have a lasting negative effect on its victims. Yet, in spite of the frequent news and greater public awareness, our children continue to be at risk.

One way to prevent abuse is to carefully educate our children, to make them aware of molesters and their lures, and to teach our children how to protect themselves. Information about abuse should be discussed with children as early as age two. Children provided with accurate information at an early age can learn to avoid or stop sexual advances. An unprepared child may be too confused or ashamed even to admit an assault has taken place.

My Body is Mine! provides a tool for addressing this delicate yet important subject with the child(ren) in your care. Read it with your child(ren) and have a discussion afterward. Conversational questions are provided at the end of the book.

Six-year-old Michael is just as nervous about attending his first sleepover party as his mom and dad are concerned for his safety. As Michael experiences being away from home for the first time, he learns critical lessons about sexual abuse, Internet dangers and self-defense.

Peter Osilaja
President and Founder
KidSafety of America

Today is my friend Andre's birthday. He is having a sleepover party and I am invited. Andre says we'll play games, watch movies and eat pizza. It sounds like it will be a lot of fun. I am so excited... and a little scared too. I have never slept at someone else's house before.

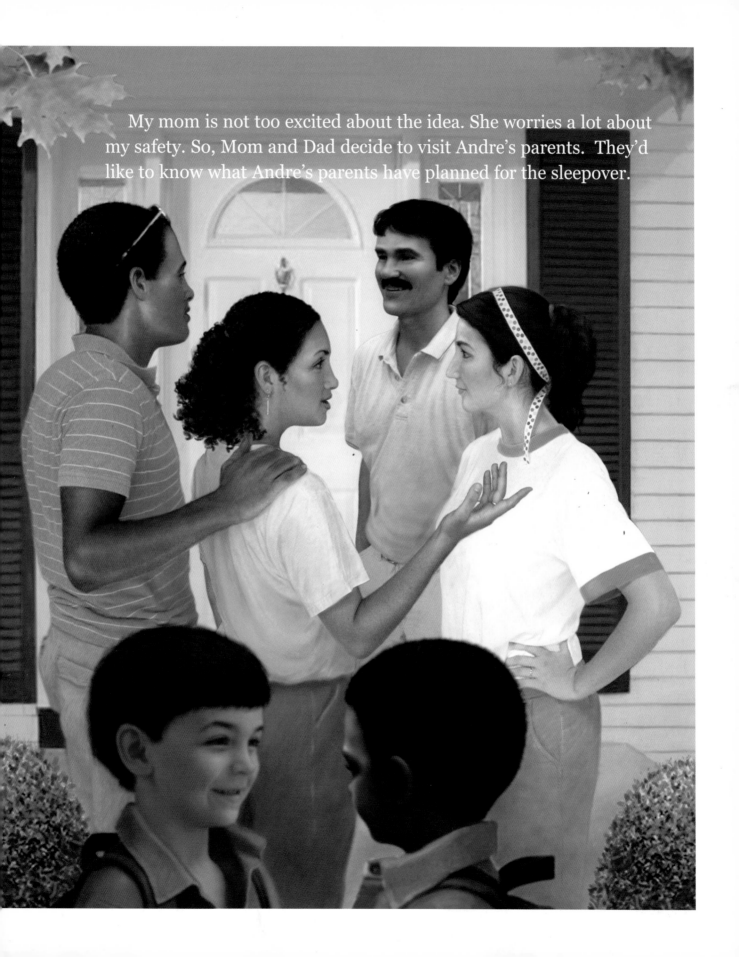

My mom is not too excited about the idea. She worries a lot about my safety. So, Mom and Dad decide to visit Andre's parents. They'd like to know what Andre's parents have planned for the sleepover.

On the way back home, they talk it over and decide to let me go to Andre's sleepover party.

We stop at a mall to pick up a birthday gift for Andre.
It's a bit boring so I act like a mannequin. I hope Andre likes his gift.

Next, we buy wrapping paper and ribbons.
At home, Mom lets me cut the ribbon while she wraps Andre's gift.
"Michael, be careful with the scissors." My dad says as he joins us.
"Did you know your body is special inside and out?" "What do you mean, inside and out?" I ask.

My dad explains, "On the inside your feelings help you to know if
something isn't right. Michael, if you ever feel afraid, confused,
angry or embarrassed, you should tell us or another trusted adult
right away."

"What about the outside?" I ask. My dad explains that every part of my body is good for something—my feet to walk, my eyes to see, my hands to hold and my nose to breathe!

"Can you think of a part of the body that is not useful?" my dad asks. Let's see, I thought. Are my knees useful? Yes. Ankles? Yes. Stomach? Yes. Ah-ha! My fingernails–they're not useful. They only collect dirt! Then I look at my mom's fingernails as she ties the ribbon on the gift. She takes such good care of them. And I love it when she scratches my back.

"No, Dad, I can't think of any part of my body that is not useful," I reply. "I must be very special from head to toe!" "And inside and out," my mom adds.

My mom asks me to take Andre's gift to my room and to rest up. As I lie on my bed, it's hard for me to sleep. I can't stop thinking of the sleepover. What will it be like? I wonder who else is coming. I like Andre, but I'm a bit scared about being away from Mom and Dad.

"Michael, it's time to take a shower and pack your overnight bag," Mom says as she walks into my room.

"Mom, I'm excited to go to Andre's house, but I'm a little scared too," I tell her. "Maybe we can talk about being safe to ease some of your fears," she says sitting on the bed beside me. She tells me that most people are very kind and safe, but there are people who are not safe to be around.

"How can I tell who is safe and who is not safe?" I ask.

"Pay attention to your feelings," she explains. "If you think something is not right, it probably isn't. No one should touch, hug or kiss you unless you give permission."

Before I take a shower, my dad joins me and talks about being safe. He tells me some things are mine and mine alone—they are private—such as my toothbrush, my underwear and my backpack.

My body is mine, too. Some parts of my body are private, and no one should touch those parts—except when I go to the doctor. Even then, my parents are with me.

"Which parts of my body are private?" I ask.

My dad explains, "Any part of your body that your underwear or swimsuit covers is private."

"If anyone should try to touch your private parts or ask you to touch his or hers, say "NO" or "STOP", then run and tell a trusted adult," he says. "This kind of behavior is a type of child abuse, and it is very unsafe."

"Dad, would I be in trouble if someone ever tried to touch me in that way?"

"Absolutely not!" Dad assures me. "It would never be your fault if someone tried to harm you."

Dad leaves the bathroom. In the shower I keep thinking about the sleepover. I am out of the shower in no time!

"Michael, let's go. Grab your stuff.
Don't forget Andre's gift," my dad calls.

I am the first to get to Andre's sleepover party.

When his other friends arrive, we play basketball for a while.

And then we chill out with snacks and drinks.

As it starts to get dark, we move inside to listen to music and play games. Andre's older sister, Megan, joins us when we start playing hide-and-seek.

Megan finds me where I am hiding. She squeezes me really tight, and I feel very uncomfortable. I tell her to stop but she doesn't, so I scream "STOP!" really loud.

Megan's dad rushes into the room to find us under the bed. "Stop squeezing Michael!" he says to Megan. After getting out from under the bed, Megan's dad then turns to me to say, "I'm glad you screamed, Michael. If someone touches you in a way that makes you feel uncomfortable, you should tell the person to stop. If the person continues, scream or run away if you can. Always tell a grown-up you can trust."

"Wow, that's the same thing my parents taught me," I tell him.

Later, we all watch a movie together.

The best part is when the door bell rings. It's the pizza guy. We all rush to the door.

Later, we ask Andre's mom if we may get on the Internet and chat with some of our friends who could not come to the party. As she helps us log on, she talks to us about staying safe, and she warns us that some people who are online may not be nice. "Some adults try to lure children when they are on the Internet."

Andre asks, "What does 'lure' mean?"

"'Lure' means to trick someone into doing something. And it's not just on the internet–some people try to lure children in person or on the phone." says Andre's mom.

"What kind of tricks do they use?" asks Paul, one of Andre's other friends.

Andre's mom tells us they might pretend to be a child our age and are very friendly. They might ask questions about private information, such as where we live and where we go to school. They might even ask for our phone number or even ask to us to meet them.

"Why do they do this?" Andre asks his mom.

She replies, "It's hard to understand what these people may be thinking, but they are dangerous and can harm you by touching you in ways that are not safe. They are called child molesters."

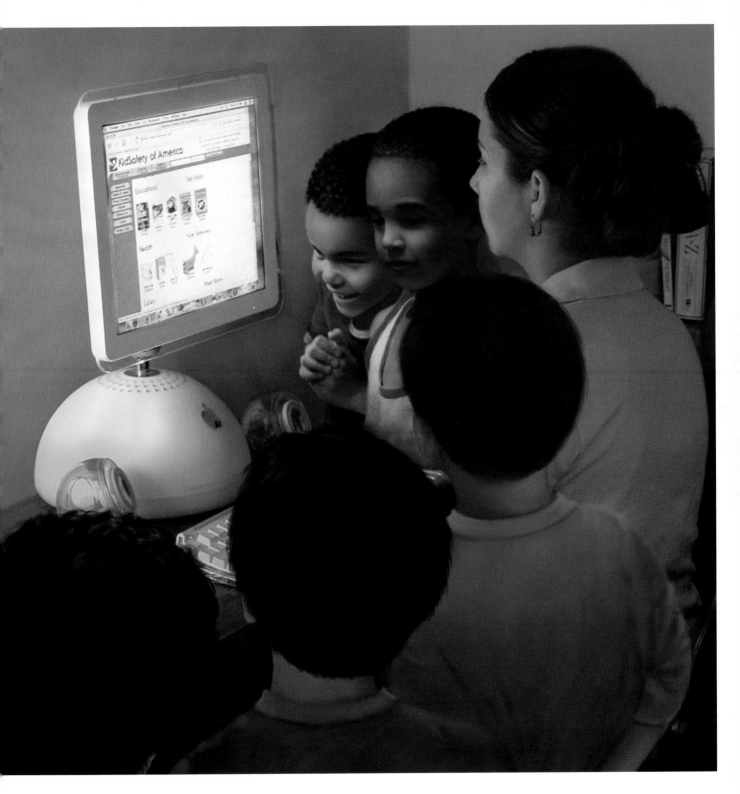

"NEVER give out your private information to strangers on the phone or the Internet," she says in a strong voice.

When Andre's mom is sure we are safely connected with our friends, she leaves the room.

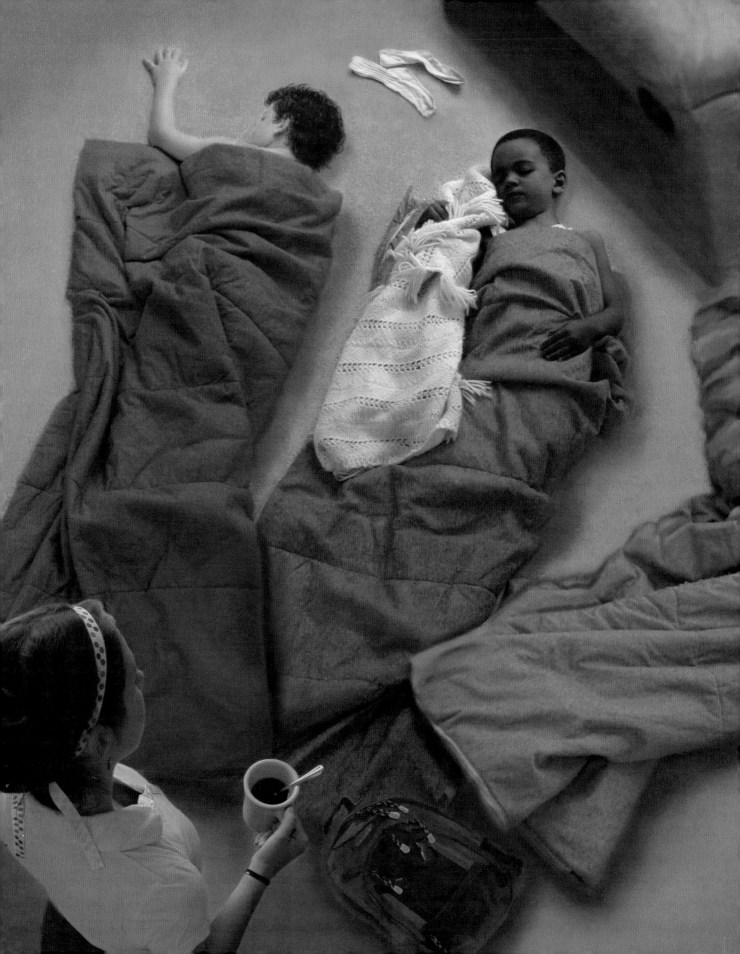

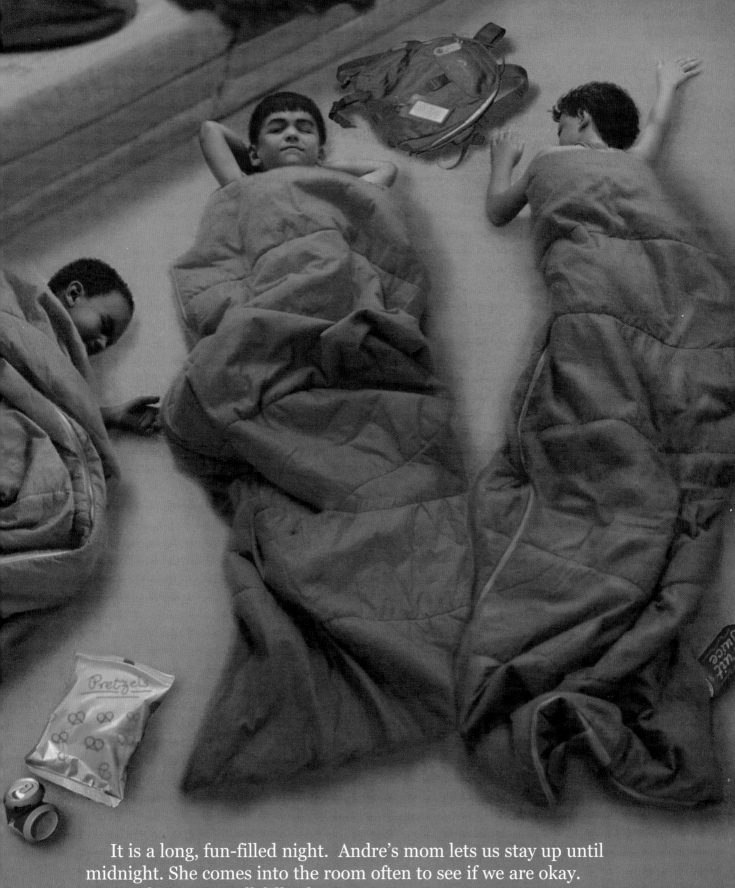

It is a long, fun-filled night. Andre's mom lets us stay up until midnight. She comes into the room often to see if we are okay. One by one, we all fall asleep.

In the morning, my mom picks me up. I am very tired and sleepy. "Are you okay?" she asks. I smile and nod, too tired to answer.

Later that day, after having a good nap, I tell my parents all about the sleepover, including the safety lessons I learned from Andre's parents. They are very pleased.

My mom has me sign a thank-you card for Andre and his parents. On Monday, after school, we drop off the card at the post office.

This past weekend was a lot of fun. I also learned a lot about how to keep myself safe. I hope you learned how to stay safe too.

DEDICATION:

This book is dedicated to the children in Africa plagued by malnutrition and AIDS.

A portion of the proceeds goes to help these children.

DISCUSSION QUESTIONS:

Dear parent, educator or caregiver,

Use the following questions to engage in discussion wih your child(ren) after reading the book together:

Have you ever stayed at someone else's house overnight?

How did you feel about going?

Why do you think Michael was feeling a little scared?

What did Michael's parents do to make sure the party was a safe place to go?

What lessons did Michael learn about safety from his parents?

How did he use what he learned over at Andre's house?

Do you like to go on the Internet? What do you like best about going on the internet?

What did Andre's mom say to the kids about adults who try to lure children on the Internet?

What Internet safety lessons did Andre's mom teach them?

Do you know that you, too, are special inside and out?

Repeat after me:

"I am special inside and out."

"I trust my feelings."

"My body is mine!"

Compiled by
Teresa Dominguez
Safe Environment Coordinator
Archdiocese of Fresno, California

RESOURCES & REFERRALS

Learn more about child abuse and neglect • Seek assistance • Support prevention efforts • Help Africa's children.

www.childwelfare.gov
Child Welfare Information Gateway. Formerly the National Clearinghouse on Child Abuse and Neglect Information

www.acf.dhhs.gov/acf_services.html#caan
U.S. Department of Health & Human Services. Administration for Children and Families. Services for Families.

www.childhelp.org
Treatment, prevention and research of child abuse and neglect. Organization also operates a hotline for child abuse and neglect.

www.preventchildabuse.org
Prevent Child Abuse America was established in 1972 to build a nationwide commitment to preventing all forms of child abuse.

www.missingkids.com
National Center for Missing and Exploited Children. Search for missing children, view wanted posters, submit child "sightings" and more.

www.kidshealth.org
Sponsored by Nemours Foundation, KidsHealth is the largest and most-visited site on the web providing doctor-approved health information about children.

www.africare.org
A leading nonprofit organization specializing in aid to Africa.

www.africaid.org
A nonprofit organization that enhances the quality of life in under-privileged African communities through sustainable development initiatives.